Reconciliation

Lenten Season Sermon Outlines

And Program Ideas

Karen Helsel

CSS Publishing Company, Inc., Lima, Ohio

RECONCILIATION
LENTEN SEASON SERMON OUTLINES AND PROGRAM IDEAS

ISBN 0-7880-1354-8

To my supportive family:
Marvin, Phil, Sharon, and Casey

Reconciliation

Sermon Outlines
For
Lenten Season

Sermon Outline 1

Topic: Reconciliation — Why Do We Need It?

Possible Texts: Genesis 3; Romans 5

Introduction: "Reconciliation" indicates that something which used to be *together* is no longer together. It has been separated and needs to be reunited. God's relationship with His creation was in such a state. How could such a thing happen and who could repair it?

A. The relationship between God and His Creation:

1. God made humans in His own image and called them "good."

Genesis 2:27-31 tells us that God made man and woman in His own image and called them "good." They were given several vital responsibilities: to be fruitful and increase in number; to rule over the earth and other creatures; and to cultivate the land, growing plants and food on the earth. They were also created for God's pleasure, to be a delight to God as they lived in relationship with Him.

2. God walked and talked with Adam and Eve in the garden.

When God created Adam and Eve, He placed them in a garden where they were to live. God walked in the garden in the cool of the day and spoke to them. Just imagine those conversations! These first people had no previous experiences on which to draw. The plants and animals that surrounded them were totally unknown to them. Perhaps as God walked and talked with Adam and Eve, He explained His creation and how it worked ... the various aquatic systems, the solar system, the ecosystems, and the natural laws He had built into each one. And then God gave them the path they were to follow to live successfully in His garden.

3. God gave guidelines for living in relationship with Him.
To live in relationship with God in the way He planned, Adam
and Eve had very specific guidelines. In Genesis 2:16-17, God
forbade Adam to partake of only one part of this lush vegeta-
tion ... the fruit from the Tree of the Knowledge of Good and
Evil. All other parts of the garden were to be enjoyed and uti-
lized for mankind's benefit. Living within this one constraint
allowed Adam and Eve to maintain a vital relationship with
their Creator.

B. The break in relationship:
1. Adam and Eve chose to go their own way.
From the moment God gave the command not to eat of the
Tree of the Knowledge of Good and Evil, Satan recognized his
opportunity. The one prohibition would become so enticing
that Adam and Eve would not refuse it. Satan first planted the
seed of doubt in Eve's mind, in Genesis 3:1, when he said,
"Did God really say ...?" And just like children told *not* to touch
something dangerous, this fruit was the very thing Eve desired.
When she realized that indeed she did not physically die upon
eating it, she gave some to Adam, and he joined in her
disobedience.

**2. This self-centered style of living continued to succeed-
ing generations.**
Today we share much the same problem as our ancestors. We
continue to desire to go our own way, do our own thing, and
hope for the best in the end. If we do find God's perfect plan
for our lives, we often see it as too constrictive and difficult,
and we seek an easier way. We want to live as we want to live
and enjoy all the pleasures available, while telling God we want
to do what He desires. Ultimately, we find ourselves in a place
similar to that of Adam and Eve — separated from the Creator
and at odds with His universe. What can we do?

C. God's plan to fix the rift:

1. The gap created by the self-centered living of God's creations.

Disobedience always leads to distance between two parties. Trust is broken; shame and guilt take its place. When a child disobeys a parent, he or she suddenly becomes more and more unavailable. There is little conversation; instead there is the inability to look squarely into the parent's eyes. When Adam and Eve disobeyed, they no longer wanted to walk and talk with God. They hid from Him. The guilt and shame they felt came between them and God and created a barrier ... a large gulf across which they could not go.

2. Jesus, God's Son, given as a sacrifice to bridge the gap.

God already had a plan to buy back this fallen creation. In Genesis 3:15, He revealed some of that plan to the serpent when He prophesied the coming of Jesus Christ. It was Jesus who would be sent to purchase our redemption by His own death on the cross for our sins.

An old story is told about a child who, with the help of his father, built a toy boat. When it was finished, they drove to the big lake near their home to try it out. Holding tightly to the rope, the boy walked along the shore and proudly watched his creation bobbing up and down on the waves. Suddenly a violent gust of wind surrounded him and tore the rope from his little hands. His father rushed to help, but it was too late. The boat was already far out in the water. The boy and his father turned sadly around and went home. Several months later, the child was walking home through the downtown shops. In a store window, he was shocked to see his very own boat for sale. He rushed in and asked the man about the boat. Indeed, it had been found and refurbished, and he could buy it for a certain amount. The child sped home to tell his father about the find and to ask if they could possibly afford to buy the boat. They returned together and purchased their very own creation.

This is what Christ did for His creation by His death on Calvary. He redeemed His very own creation from the hands of the enemy.

Conclusion: Before we can accept the solution to a problem, we must recognize that there is indeed a problem. God's plan is in place; He is prepared to be reconciled to His creation, and He has taken the first drastic steps. As we spend time during this Lenten season in personal reflection, let us understand how distant we have grown from our Heavenly Father, and how much He wants to be back in fellowship with us. Let us take positive steps toward Him to complete the plan of our reconciliation.

Sermon Outline 2

Topic: Our Need For Reconciliation With Ourselves

Possible Texts: John 13:1-17; Romans 7:14-24

Introduction: Romans 7 indicates the dichotomy which exists within the heart of every believer. Those things we deeply desire to do, we find impossible, while those things we detest are the very ones we find ourselves doing. Where is willpower and self-control? Rather than being a case of strength versus weakness, the answer may lie in finding our true selves and allowing God's Spirit to transform us.

A. Jesus knew Himself:
1. He knew where He came from and where He was going. From a very young age, Jesus seemed to understand that He had a higher purpose in life. At the age of twelve, He accompanied His parents on the annual trip to Jerusalem for the celebration of the Passover Feast. When His parents left to return home, Jesus stayed behind to talk with the religious leaders. When His parents finally found Him at the temple, He seemed perplexed that His parents did not understand what He was doing. "Didn't you know I had to be in my Father's house?" He asked them. It is difficult to ascertain for sure what exactly Jesus understood to be His mission at this point. It seems apparent, however, that He was compelled, drawn, called to sit and talk about the things of His heavenly Father. He knew the fascination of the spiritual and it was shaping His life. As He grew older and experienced both His home life and time at the synagogue, there was likely a growing awareness that His time at home was nearing an end, and that He must soon begin the ministry for which He came. As He experienced baptism by John, God's power and full knowledge of who He was was confirmed within Him. He knew for certain what He was called to do, and He gave himself totally to His call. Throughout His time on earth, Jesus spent a great deal of time talking to His

10

heavenly Father. It was likely during these times that He was made more and more aware of His heavenly connection, His roots, His origin. And He knew that the Father was in control of all that was happening in His life.

2. This knowledge allowed Him to humble Himself to do the task of a slave.

Jesus did not try to prove He was God's Son. None of His miracles were done for self-aggrandizement or self-justification. He *knew* who He was. Nobody could take that knowledge from Him. No task He did, no service He performed could negate the fact that He was the Creator, Redeemer, God's Son. So He could willingly serve, without seeking any kind of accolades or praise. He recognized that His real praise and honor came from His Father. Doing the Father's will was the most vital part of His life.

B. Who does *God* say we are? Finding our true identity is a vital task.

Psychologists have listed it as a key work of adolescence. We receive input from many sources: parents, grandparents, teachers, siblings, the church, and our peers. Society also gives us messages about who we are. Sometimes these are conflicting messages, and we have trouble understanding who we really are.

1. Redeemed children of God.

In 1 Peter (1:18-19), we are reminded that we were redeemed or bought back for God by the precious blood of Jesus Christ, not with silver or gold. It was Jesus' supreme sacrifice of Himself on the cross that allows us to be in relationship with the Heavenly Father once again.

2. Adopted, chosen by Him.

God's work through Jesus Christ means that we have been chosen. Adoption is a very special process ... of choosing. And when the process is complete, the chosen one becomes an intimate part of the family, with full rights and privileges of natural-born children. Paul, in his letter to the Galatians, explains this spiritual adoption program to them in chapter 4 verses 3-7: "So also, when we were children, we were in slavery under the basic principles of the world. But when the time had fully come, God sent his Son, born of a woman, born under law, to redeem those under law, that we might receive the full rights of sons. Because you are sons, God sent the Spirit of his Son into our hearts, the Spirit who calls out 'Abba, Father.' So you are no longer a slave, but a son; and since you are a son, God has made you also an heir." Because of Christ's gift of salvation to us, we have been chosen as God's children.

3. Beloved — He delights in us.
God's heart is turned to us ... He loves us. John, the beloved disciple of Jesus, reminds us in his first epistle, "How great is the love the Father has lavished on us, that we should be called children of God! And that is what we are!" He loved us so much that He was willing to do whatever it took to reconcile us to Himself. We are His beloved.

C. **Accepting God's truth about ourselves encourages us to be reconciled to the person God created us to be:**
    1. Affirm what God says ... *act as if.*
    Alcoholics Anonymous has been the key to recovery for millions of persons over the years. Even though it may not be suitable for everyone, it continues to bring hope to many. Part of the reason for the success of this program is that it helps people connect with Someone greater than themselves to help in their fight. Integral to an AA program is the idea of living one day at a time, affirming new truths about oneself. At first people are encouraged to "act as if" these affirmations were true, because they are not always able to believe good things about themselves. The longer they use this tool, the more convinced they become of it.

    When God says to us, "You are dearly loved children of Mine," we may at first have to "act as if" it is true. As we do

12

so, we will often find ourselves replacing old, negative thinking with new, more positive thoughts about ourselves.

2. Play new "tapes" if the childhood ones are faulty.
All of us have within the recesses of our minds tapes that we have heard all our lives. Some of the messages are not ones we actually heard but may have merely perceived or "felt." Whether or not our perception was correct, we may have trouble taking in ideas of how God really feels about us, because we cannot escape the negative messages already residing in us. The conflict between what we know in our heads of God's love and care with what we have always believed in our minds about ourselves requires reconciliation. God wants to bring a true knowledge of His thoughts about us and a healing of past destructive thinking. Filling our minds and hearts with God's Word to us, talking with Him, spending time in worship and praise, finding His servants who will continue to affirm us, all will help us find wholeness.

An old story tells of someone asking Michelangelo how in the world he did the famous carving of David; how did he bring such an exquisite statue out of a piece of marble? Michelangelo is said to have replied, "I sat for days and stared at the stone. Then I began to chip away everything that was not David."

As we look for the truth about ourselves, God wants to help us become more and more like His original plan for us ... more and more our true selves.

Conclusion: Living as dearly beloved, redeemed children of God will bring freedom — the same kind of freedom possessed by Jesus. We will find the strength and ability to accept both our accomplishments and our failures, using them as stepping stones to further growth. We will no longer have to prove to ourselves or anyone else who we are. We will know ourselves and be able to accept God's idea of our worth and value.

13

Sermon Outline 3

Topic: Reconciliation In Our Families

Possible Texts: Excerpts from Joseph's life: Genesis 37, 39, 40-43, 45, 50 (Especially 50:15-21)

Introduction: Living together in families gives opportunity for positive interaction. It can also be the soil in which anger, bitterness, and brokenness abound. It is in families that we experience the need for reconciliation and can see God at work.

A. **Joseph's story: the fractured family.** The story of Joseph spans numerous chapters in the book of Genesis. Beginning with his birth in chapter 30, conflict and difficulties abounded in Joseph's family. The legacy of his deceptive but doting father affected the intricate relationships with his siblings. Joseph's special status as the firstborn of the beloved Rachel elicited anger and jealousy from his brothers. His brightly-colored coat was a constant reminder that he was their father's favorite. The family was fractured — but God was with Joseph.

1. Revelations (Genesis 37).
Joseph was a dreamer. His visions, vivid and remarkable, were freely shared with those around him. Even though the full meaning of his dreams was not known, they seemed to indicate to everyone who heard them that his brothers and even his father would one day bow down to him. This prediction was odious to his brothers. They plotted Joseph's destruction — but God was with Joseph and spared his life.

2. Inspired integrity.
After being sold into slavery in Egypt, Joseph became a valued slave in Potiphar's house. His was a life of luxury; he lived with power and prestige. When Potiphar's wife set her sights on Joseph, however, she was not prepared for his strong moral

character. He would not compromise his values for momentary pleasure. This landed him in prison on false charges — but God was with Joseph and God brought him back to an even greater place.

3. Consequences.

Joseph's problems were not insignificant ones. Over and over again he could have been killed. Joseph's faithfulness to his dream and his unquestioning integrity cost him comfort and status — but God was with Joseph and His plan was greater than simply saving the life of one man.

B. God's plan: God's plans are able to supersede the plans we have for our lives. He knows our possibilities and has expectations of which we have never dreamed.

1. He uses every situation to take us toward His final purposes.

Each step of Joseph's life was used by God. From the dreams to the multicolored coat, the path was paved for Joseph's brothers to act on their jealousy and hatred — but God used Joseph in Egypt. From the palace to prison and back again, Joseph's steps were ordered by God to prepare for the coming famine.

2. Reconciliation brings salvation.

The famine had spread and Joseph's family felt the effects of it back home. Jacob reluctantly sent his sons to Egypt in search of grain. There they came face to face with the brother they thought no longer existed. As realization dawned, fear gripped them. But Joseph knew. He saw how God had prepared him and placed him in a position to save his family from starvation. Genesis 50:19-21 records his words as he is reconciled with his brothers: "Don't be afraid. Am I in the place of God? You intended to harm me, but God intended it for good to accomplish what is now being done, the saving of many lives. So then, don't be afraid. I will provide for you and your children."

Conclusion: People's intentions versus God's plan ... God can bring good even out of our broken family relationships. Families today are broken in record numbers. The divorce rate in our country is approximately 65 percent; domestic violence and child abuse is on the rise at an alarming rate. Although our economy is booming, money has not been able to put us back together again.

Broken people and broken lives are God's workshop. He desires to mend and heal, to put the fractured pieces back together again. In this reconciliation, He wants to bring salvation. Will you give Him the broken pieces of your life and family?

Sermon Outline 4

Topic: Reconciliation In Your Church Family

Possible Text: Ephesians 4

Introduction: Many of Paul's epistles were written to churches which met in homes. The practical instructions he offered will enhance the life of the Family of God, as well as the physical family. Struggles exist in both the home and the church, and the path to reconciliation is basically the same.

A. **Requirements for unity (vv. 1-7):** Unity in the Body of Christ was and is a necessity. Jesus prayed for it Himself. John records this prayer in which Jesus said, "Holy Father, protect them by the power of your name — the name you gave me — so that they may be one as we are one." Unity among believers, reconciliation within the church, is God's idea. But how can it be accomplished? Paul gives some ideas which will lead us on the path to unity.

   1. Live a life worthy of a believer in Christ.
   In Ephesians 5:2, Paul goes on to describe what he means by a worthy life: "Be imitators of Christ"; "Live as dearly loved children"; "Live a life of love" as Jesus did. Jesus once told His disciples that they would attract others to faith in Him when they showed love for each other. Loving others in the Body of Christ is a basic requirement for unity, but it is not easy to do.

   Helen had been invited to a Bible study led by a missionary. Helen fled from her Communist homeland and was a bitter, unhappy woman. As she heard and read the scriptures, she loudly stated her opinions: "I don't believe a word of that." The missionary leader found herself wishing that Helen would sometimes stay home from Bible study. One day in prayer, the missionary was convicted of her lack of love for Helen. But how could she love her? Her prayer was, "Help me to *want* to love Helen, because I really don't want to." Helen was out of the country for about a month, and the missionary continued to pray for Helen and for herself. One day they chanced to meet on a busy city street. The missionary was overcome by the change she felt — a genuine love and concern for Helen.

God desires for us to love others. When we love them as Christ does, we will be able to live together more easily.

2. Be humble, gentle, and patient with each other.

This command leaves us aghast. Incredibly difficult, if not impossible, the simple statement calls us to a higher plane of living. We are to leave our vanity, our pompous pride, our biting tongues and spirits, our insatiable desire for our own immediate gratification. We are to quiet ourselves and become people of peace and unity. We can do this as we fix our eyes firmly on our example, Christ. When we begin to see people through His eyes, as He would view them, we will more easily be able to overlook the small things.

3. Make every effort to be united in peace.

We are called in Christ's Body to persevere in our pursuit of unity and peace. A single effort will not suffice. Imaginative means may need to be employed to become the church He desires. Working together to better our communities, reaching out to struggling children and single parents, building homes for low-income families ... doing things which focus us toward needs outside ourselves may aid in bringing us closer together.

Although we are to make every effort to be unified in peace, this does not mean we are to be uniform. We are not being called to become carbon copies of each other. In fact, diversity brings abundant benefits.

B. **Our diversity leads to maturity (vv. 11-16):** Along the Oregon beaches are many unique stones, all shapes and colors. One such native stone is the agate. At first glance, the agate doesn't look like much. Place the agates in a tumbling machine, however, and allow them to bump against each other, and the result is exquisite beauty. Sharp edges are smoothed, rough places disappear, and each stone glows with a breathtaking shine.

Putting the different members of the Body together can also have a positive effect on each member, resulting in spiritual growth and maturity ... God's idea.

1. Different leadership gifts benefit the whole Body of Christ.

God provided for leadership in the church by appointing persons with a variety of gifts. All are vital to the working of the Body. Apostles, prophets, evangelists, pastors, and teachers are the gifted leaders to guide the church as it strives to live and grow together.

Today people have different gifts in the church. When a person uses his or her gifts, the work of the Kingdom is enhanced. When a person chooses not to use his or her gift, the church will survive. The gifted person, however, may miss an opportunity for service and spiritual growth.

A woman in a local parish knew that she was gifted in the area of administration. She was able to inspire, plan and prepare, and lead others. When she used her gifts, others responded by using their gifts as well. Her ability to motivate others to share their gifts impacted a great number of persons.

2. Gifts are given to prepare God's people to serve and become mature.

God's goal for the church is that believers be built up in faith and knowledge as they serve one another. The gifted leadership of the church focuses on preparing God's people for works of service so that spiritual growth may result.

Another parishioner was a gifted teacher. When he led a Bible class, people became excited about reading the scripture. His class was full of people engaging in lively discussion each week. Others in his class recognized their own gifts of teaching while participating in his class. They went on to lead other groups in the church. God's gifts are to be used to prepare the Body of Christ to serve one another.

C. **Practical guides for living together (vv. 17-32):** Paul becomes proactive toward the end of this chapter. He does not want simply to wait until there are problems or conflicts in the Body. His practical advice is given to help ward off possible difficulties which could arise.

1. Change the way you think.

Paul's admonition to guard carefully our thinking is of vital importance to believers in our times. We are bombarded with a plethora of opportunities for entertainment which not only dull our senses, but may bring enormous harm. Our minds have been subtly desensitized to accept input that we might previously have rejected. The television and movie industry carefully strategizes to utilize our subconscious mind.

A junior high teacher questioned some students to see if they felt they were affected by television commercials. They insisted they were not. Twenty advertising jingles were read, with the product name missing. All but one product was immediately named. "Programming" means far more than just the lineup of shows on a network. Our minds are also being "programmed" to accept things we do not find acceptable. We are slowly but surely being desensitized to damaging material.

It is like the successful method for killing a frog. If one catches a frog and immediately places it in a pan of boiling water, the frog will waste no time jumping to safety. If, however, the frog is placed in a pan of cool water, it will stay. When the burner is turned on, and the water begins to heat, the frog will never know what hit him ... he will not be able to escape.

Paul's admonition to regain our sensitivity, to put away deceitful desires, and allow Christ to renew our minds is desperately needed. As we fill our minds and hearts with God's Word, with uplifting reading, entertainment, and fellowship, we will be strengthened in our spirits.

2. Be careful with your anger.

Paul does not say to avoid anger all together. Anger is a God-given emotion, which often leads to positive actions and changes. Paul is saying here to control our anger rather than letting it control us. When we harbor anger and allow it to become bitterness and resentment, Paul says we open the door to the dividing work of Satan.

Nothing delights Satan more than to see church members fighting and bickering about issues. He watches for and creates factions in the church. It is in these places of discord that his work is most easily accomplished. Anger then becomes a fuel for the fires of discontent and separation.

Anger, however, can be used to bring people together around a common cause. It can motivate people to put aside smaller differences of opinion to join in fighting a greater problem, enhancing the process of reconciliation in the church.

3. Watch what you say: build up and encourage.

Finally, Paul reminds us to be careful about the words we use. Words have the power to build others up or to destroy. James uses vivid illustrations about the power of our speech: like a bit in a horse's mouth or like a rudder on a huge ship, our tongue is very powerful.

To facilitate reconciliation in the Body of Christ, we can look for ways to speak words of encouragement to other believers. Refusing to listen to gossip and spread it further will inspire positive attitudes and speech. We are able to put out "fires" that could otherwise be spread by inflammatory words. Thanking others and praising them for what they do lifts spirits and brings peace. The scripture constantly calls us to be peacemakers in our words and deeds, calling for reconciliation in the Body of Christ.

Conclusion: Which difficult relationships in the Body of Christ could be healed if we followed Paul's prescription? What is God calling you to do today to make positive changes in His church? How can you use your giftedness to bring unity and reconciliation to God's people and to help them grow and mature? In what areas have you been challenged to be renewed by Christ?

Sermon Outline 5

Topic: Reconciliation In The Community

Possible Text: Acts 10

Introduction: The early believers were convinced that the gospel was for the Jews. They were God's chosen people, through whom the Messiah had come. But God was expanding the Kingdom and would shake up their preconceived ideas in order to complete His plan.

A. **The story — Acts 10:** Persecution in the early church had scattered believers to many other cities. Peter had become an itinerant encourager and preacher, visiting Christians in various locations. He was staying in Joppa where he had already seen God raise a woman from death. God was about to surprise Peter in another way.

   1. Cornelius' call.
   Cornelius was the captain of Roman soldiers in Caesarea, a town just north of Joppa. He was a person of influence as well as a God-fearing, devout man and a Gentile. Part of his tradition included times of prayer and worship. It was during one of these times of prayer that he had a vision of an angel, who told him to send to Joppa and ask Peter to come and share with him and his family. Although the angel gave Cornelius no details about Peter's visit, Cornelius obeyed.

   2. Stretching Peter's parameters.
   God prepared Peter, too, for his new outreach. His vision, as he prayed on the rooftop, astounded and perplexed him. Three times a sheet was let down from heaven filled with both clean and unclean animals. Peter was given the command to kill and eat. And three times Peter refused, claiming that he had never disobeyed the Jewish ceremonial laws regarding specific foods he was to eat. God explodes Peter's ideas when He reminds

Peter that nothing He has made pure is unclean. (See Leviticus 11 for lists of clean and unclean animals.)

When the vision was completed, Peter ruminated on what its possible meanings were until the Holy Spirit spoke to him. Three men were at the door at that moment, and he was to go with them because God had sent them. Peter was to visit a Gentile home.

Entering a Gentile home was forbidden for the Jews, much less eating there. They felt that Gentiles were extremely careless about the foods they ate. A Jew could be ceremonially unclean by even touching some utensils which might have been used for certain foods.

Peter was amazed at God's plan, but he participated and witnessed the Spirit's movement among His people. In verses 34-35 he confessed, "I now realize how true it is that God does not show favoritism but accepts men from every nation who fear him and do what is right."

B. **Differences in our community:** We are a people who naturally separate ourselves from others. We do so on the basis of many different criteria.

1. Poverty versus wealth.

The economy has been booming in our country for some time. Ups and downs have come, but "strong" is the word most often used to describe the economic trends. Unemployment has been down as well as inflation. However, the percentage of homeless people has increased. How can that be? Although there are some good things happening, there is still a great discrepancy between the rich and the poor.

A social worker was sharing about a ministry to homeless women at a local service club whose membership was mostly professional people. At the end of her talk, she opened the floor for questions. "How do these women get to this point?" "Don't they have families?" "Have they been on drugs or alcohol?" "What's their problem?" Their voices betrayed their incredulity at the plight of the poor. Somehow the poor seemed "less than," not as valuable. It was difficult for them to relate to or empathize with the needy.

2. Racial divisions.
Although we may insist that problems were solved by the civil rights movement, we are still very divided over race. Churches, communities, and social institutions across parts of our country continue to portray our separateness. Subtle racist attitudes are felt by many today.

Some time ago a television show dealt with this issue. A young black man was made up to be white and went shopping first as a white person and then as a black person — in the same stores. A video camera caught the obvious shift in treatment he received.

3. Religious walls of separation.
Unity of believers was the prayer of Christ. And yet His Body, the church, is broken into thousands of pieces. Competition for members and money seems to often override the desire to take the message of salvation to all people. Instead of watching the church down the street with joy and thanksgiving as they grow, we may look with suspicion on programs and people. Building walls to protect our flocks often absorbs more time than feeding the flock.

C. **God's inclusive plan:** God can never be kept in a box. He works through traditions and history, but He is also an innovative, creative God. He is willing to do whatever it takes to bring all people into His Kingdom.

1. He destroys barriers that separate people.
Paul, in his letter to the church at Ephesus, writes about the demolition of the wall between Jew and Gentile: "For he himself is our peace, who has made the two one and has destroyed the barrier, the dividing wall of hostility, by abolishing in his flesh the law with its commandments and regulations. His purpose was to create in himself one new man out of the two, thus

making peace, and in this one body to reconcile both of them to God through the cross, by which he put to death their hostility" (Ephesians 2:14-16).

Jesus' death on the cross broke down the barrier between Jew and Gentile. It is His death on the cross which also helps break down other walls we have built. As we meet together at the foot of the cross with those who are different than we are, our differences melt away in the presence of the crucified Christ.

2. He desires that all persons hear the message of reconciliation.

God's message of reconciliation is not for a chosen few. John, the beloved disciple, used the word, "whoever." Whoever received, whoever believed, would be included in this reconciliation with Jesus Christ.

If we are to share the good news with others, we must begin to break down the walls that separate us. We must seek to work together, share together, understand each other, and pray for each other.

Conclusion: Will you join together as we pray for reconciliation in our community? Will you each represent the diversity of religious denominations, social classes, races, gender, and other differences? As we pray, will you commit yourself to work together to share the message of reconciliation across all lines?

Sermon Outline 6

Topic: Reconciliation In The World

Possible Texts: Revelation 7:9-17; Matthew 28:19-20

Introduction: God's plan is infinitely larger than our plans. We might share the message of reconciliation with our own family, local congregation, denomination, or community. But God wants the whole world to know He desires to be reconciled with them. Our task is daunting.

A. **The brokenness of our world — examples from our society:** We live in a time when news is flashed around the world within seconds. No longer are we aware of only the tragedies in our local communities; the world is at our doorstep and in our living rooms. We may not have been to Africa, but starving children have stared at us in our parlors. We were not in Paris when Princess Diana lost her life, but the accident played out in our homes. Terrorist bombs shatter lives in other parts of the globe, and our peace is somehow shaken. When a financial crisis hits the Asian stock market, the reaction is felt worldwide.

 We live in a time when the pain and agony of people in faraway places can easily be known to us. We may even find ourselves wishing we could turn back the clock; it would be easier *not* to know. Our world is broken and hurting. And God's heart breaks with it.

B. **God's vision:** God's vision is a worldwide one. Beyond our capacity truly to understand, His view is panoramic. The gospel of reconciliation is for people everywhere.

1. Every group is represented before His throne.
In John's record of the revelations he received from God, we continue to experience God's expansive plans. In verse 9 John says, "After this I looked and there before me was a great

26

multitude that no one could count, from every nation, tribe, people, and language, standing before the throne and in front of the Lamb." How many groups was that?

There are missionaries today sharing the gospel in the far corners of our world because they believe this vision is God's plan. Chinese, Kazakh, Maasi, Prai, Jamaican, Peruvian, on and on ... people we have never met are hearing the gospel and responding to the call to be reconciled to their Creator.

Can you imagine the scene as John saw it? One day we will stand with these brothers and sisters. We will all be speaking different languages. We will have uniquely shaped faces and skin of various hues. But our focus will be the same: Jesus Christ.

2. Christ is the center of our reconciliation and our unity.
It is Christ who is the focal point of our coming together with believers from all over the world. Christ gave His life in order to reconcile all people everywhere to their Father, God. It is He who has the power to make us one through His Spirit. As we place Him at the center of our lives and our world, we will put aside the differences in our culture, language, and lifestyles, and we will worship Him together.

C. **God calls us to share the message of reconciliation with our world:** So, what is our responsibility to people throughout our world? In Romans chapter 10, Paul says, "How, then, can they call on the one they have not believed in? And how can they believe in the one of whom they have not heard? And how can they hear without someone preaching to them? And how can they preach unless they are sent?"

1. Be a "sender" — give, equip, encourage.
There is a great need today for people who will "send" others to share the gospel in the world. There are so many charities and causes offering us a place to give our money. We have a great responsibility to be educated about the opportunities and the organizations doing the work of mission in our world. Where

will our gifts equip and encourage the most? How can we free up money to share the gospel?

We may not have money to give, but we may be able to write letters or send e-mail messages of encouragement to those who are working in other lands. We may be able to share resources of books, tapes, or other needed materials. We can all be intercessors in prayer for those we send, calling on God for their protection, wisdom, and peace. But God may be asking for more.

2. Go yourself and tell the message.

God may be asking us to go ourselves ... Jesus instructed the disciples to begin to share the gospel in Jerusalem, then Judea and Samaria, and then the world. We may sometimes find it easier to write a check to support missions in another country, rather than tell our neighbors about how Jesus can meet their needs. When we begin to see God at work in the people with whom we share, we will be inspired to share even more. We may even find ourselves going beyond our neighborhood.

Mission trips to other parts of the world are excellent opportunities to broaden our spiritual horizons, to meet other people of God with whom we will share eternity. We can educate ourselves to know better how to give, equip, and encourage. Many persons who now serve in foreign mission fields first participated in a mission trip to increase their awareness of the needs of the world.

Conclusion: God's plan for the reconciliation of all humanity is far beyond our comprehension. It requires the personal involvement of all who name the name of Christ. Christ's command to go and make disciples was to all of us. In one way or another, we are to go and tell the world the message of His love and grace, His reconciliation.

Reconciliation

Program Ideas
For
Lenten Season

"Fat Tuesday"

"Fat Tuesday" (the day before Ash Wednesday) was traditionally a time of celebration and feasting in preparation for the season of Lent. Plan a church carry-in dinner and social hour on the Sunday evening prior to Lent. It should be an evening of fun and laughter.

Program ideas:
1. A "talent(less) night" with skits, music, readings, and other "talents" shared by members of the congregation. Invite anyone and everyone to participate as time allows.
2. Humorous drama put on by youth or members of the congregation, or bring in a special guest.
3. Christian concert.

Other ideas:

Coordinator:

Planning schedule:

Family Reconciliation Workshop

This event could be held in conjunction with the emphasis on reconciliation in the family.

As a half-day event to encourage families of all kinds to experience healing and togetherness, this workshop could be led by a guest counselor or pastor. The goal would be to offer special tools and resources to help families work toward healthy relationships.

Some suggested topics:
- Humor in the Home
- Journaling for Healing
- Examining the Family Tree, Working a Genogram
- Visioning Praying: Healing Past Hurts with Christ

Caution: In a half-day seminar, there is not sufficient time to do in-depth counseling work. A counselor or pastor could give instruction and practice in using two or three tools that people could use. Creating resource packets containing books, tapes, names, and numbers of Christian counselors in the area would be beneficial.

Other ideas:

Coordinator:

Planning schedule:

Palm Sunday

Palm Sunday procession into the sanctuary ... children and choir joining in singing praises. Palm branches could be laid at the foot of the cross at the end of the procession.

The dramatic reading from Mark 15:1-37 is an effective bridge from the party atmosphere of Palm Sunday to the solemnity of Holy Week. (See Worship Aids and Dramatic Reading.)

Other ideas:

Coordinator:

Planning schedule:

Maundy Thursday Service

This service commemorates the Last Supper and will include a communion service in the style observed by individual congregations. Some congregations may want to vary the venue: move from the chapel into a room where tables can be placed in the U-shape. Communion could be served by the pastor or priest from within the U-shaped space.

To follow through on the theme of reconciliation, footwashing participants are invited to share insights from the *Lenten Season Worship and Study Guide*. One variation: ask participants to identify someone or some group with whom they have discovered they need reconciliation. They may then ask someone in the room to represent that person or group and allow the participant to wash their feet. Songs of thanksgiving and humility are appropriate to this setting and service.

Other ideas:

Coordinator:

Planning schedule:

Good Friday and Easter Celebrations

With long-range planning, both of these celebrations are very effective when many churches are brought together from a variety of traditions in a community-wide observance. The texture of the celebrations is rich as people from different denominations focus together on their common belief, the death and resurrection of Jesus Christ. The use of drama, music, and preaching will enhance these special days. (See Dramatic Reading from Mark 15:1-37.)

Other ideas:

Coordinator:

Planning schedule:

Reconciliation

Worship Aids
And
Dramatic Reading

Worship Aids

On the first Sunday of Lent, a pitcher, basin, and towel are brought to the front of the sanctuary and placed on a small table. They remain for the season of Lent as a symbol of the spirit of reconciliation, seen in the act of servanthood when Jesus washed His disciples' feet.

Each Sunday thereafter, a tableau depicting the washing of feet takes place during part of the service, utilizing various persons to symbolize humility. For instance, a boss and an employee, a husband and wife, an African-American youth and a Caucasian woman could participate on different Sundays. During the tableau, the couple would exchange places, so that each depicts washing the other's feet.

An effective song used during the tableau is "The Reconciliation Song," words and music by Morris Chapman, Buddy Owens, and Claire Cloninger. Copyright 1995 Word Music. (Available through Promise Keepers.)

Dramatic Reading From Mark 15:1-37

Reader 1: As soon as it was morning, the chief priests held a consultation with the elders and scribes and the whole council. They bound Jesus, led him away, and handed him over to Pilate. Pilate asked him,

Reader 2: "Are you the King of the Jews?"

Reader 1: He answered him,

Reader 2: "You say so."

Reader 1: Then the chief priests accused him of many things. Pilate asked him again,

Reader 2: "Have you no answer? See how many charges they bring against you."

Reader 1: But Jesus made no further reply, so that Pilate was amazed. Now at the festival he used to release a prisoner for them, anyone for whom they asked. Now a man called Barabbas was in prison with the rebels who had committed murder during the insurrection. So the crowd came and began to ask Pilate to do for them according to his custom. Then he answered them,

Reader 2: "Do you want me to release for you the King of the Jews?"

Reader 1: For he realized that it was out of jealousy that the chief priests had handed him over. But the chief priests stirred up the crowd to have him release Barabbas for them instead. Pilate spoke to them again,

Reader 2: "Then what do you wish me to do with the man you call the King of the Jews?"

Reader 1: They shouted back,

People: "Crucify him! Crucify him! CRUCIFY HIM!"

Reader 1: Pilate asked them,

Reader 2: "Why, what evil has he done?"

Reader 1: But they shouted all the more,

People: "Crucify him! Crucify him! CRUCIFY HIM!"

Reader 1: So Pilate, wishing to satisfy the crowd, released Barabbas for them; and after flogging Jesus, he handed him over to be crucified. Then the soldiers led him into the courtyard of the palace (that is, the governor's headquarters); and they called together the whole cohort. And they clothed him in a purple cloak; and after twisting some thorns into a crown, they put it on him. And they began saluting him,

People: "Hail, King of the Jews!"

Reader 1: They struck his head with a reed, spat upon him, and knelt down in homage to him. After mocking him, they stripped him of the purple cloak and put his own clothes on him. Then they led him out to crucify him. They compelled a passerby, who was coming in from the country, to carry his cross; it was Simon of Cyrene, the father of Alexander and Rufus. Then they brought Jesus to the place called Golgotha (which means the place of a skull). And they offered him wine mixed with myrrh; but he did not take it. And they crucified him, and divided his clothes among them, casting lots to decide what each should take. It was nine o'clock in the morning when they crucified him. The inscription of the charge against him read, "The King of the Jews." And with him they crucified two bandits, one on his right and one on his left. Those who passed by derided him, shaking their heads and saying,

People: "Aha! You who would destroy the temple and build it in three days, save yourself, and come down from the cross!"

Reader 1: In the same way the chief priests, along with the scribes, were also mocking him among themselves and saying,

Reader 2: "He saved others; he cannot save himself. Let the Messiah, the King of Israel, come down from the cross now, so that we may see and believe."

Reader 1: Those who were crucified with him also taunted him. When it was noon, darkness came over the whole land until three in the afternoon. At three o'clock Jesus cried out with a loud voice,

Reader 2: *"Eloi, Eloi, lema sabachthani?"*

Reader 1: which means,

Reader 2: "My God, my God, why have you forsaken me?"

Reader 1: When some of the bystanders heard it, they said,

People: "Listen, he is calling for Elijah."

Reader 1: And someone ran, filled a sponge with sour wine, put it on a stick, and gave it to him to drink, saying,

Reader 2: "Wait, let us see whether Elijah will come to take him down."

Reader 1: Then Jesus gave a loud cry and breathed his last.

(From *The Holy Bible*, New Revised Standard Version, Zondervan Publishing House, Grand Rapids, Michigan, 1989.)